What the Cluck

A Tongue-in-Beak View of the World

Written and Illustrated by Sarah Rosedahl

Sarah Rosedahl

ISBN-13:978-0692974322 (Tolba Farm Press)
ISBN-10:0692974326

DEDICATED TO THE FIRST AMENDMENT

Congress shall make no law respecting an establishment of religion, or prohibiting the free exercise thereof; or abridging the freedom of speech, or of the press; or the right of the people peaceably to assemble, and to petition the Government for a redress of grievances.

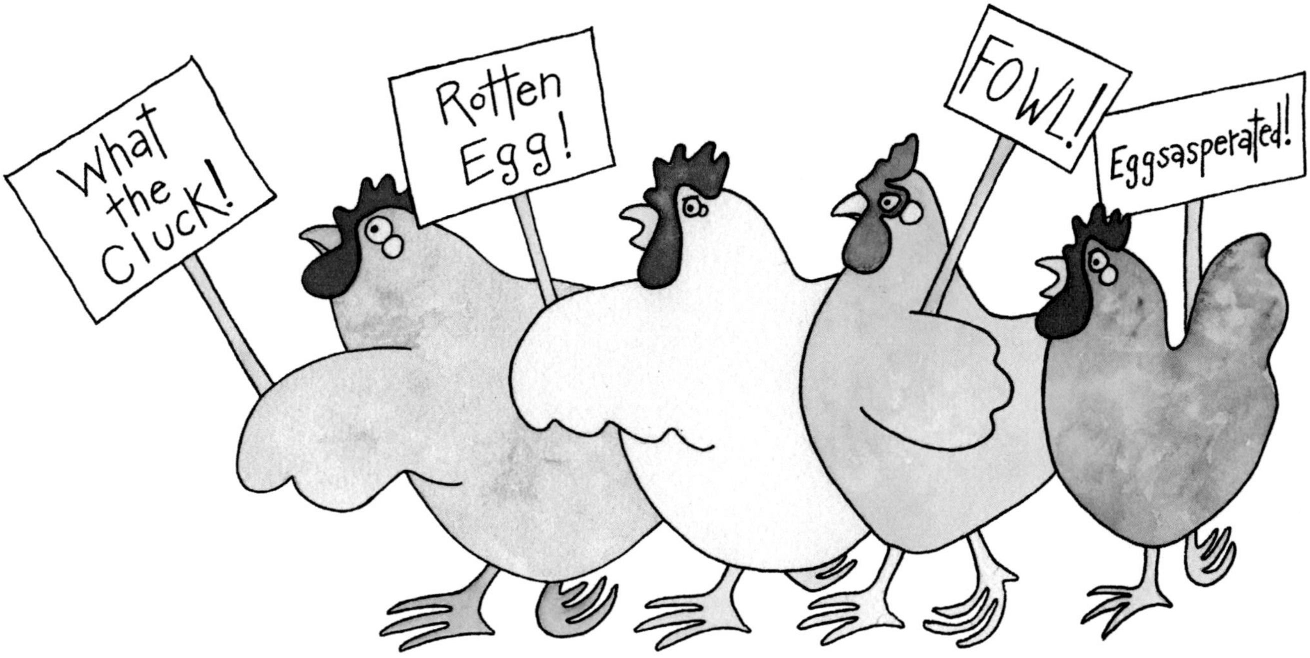
What the Cluck!
Rotten Egg!
FOWL!
Eggsasperated!

SARAH'S HAT

" The most courageous act is still
to think for yourself. Aloud."

        – Coco Chanel

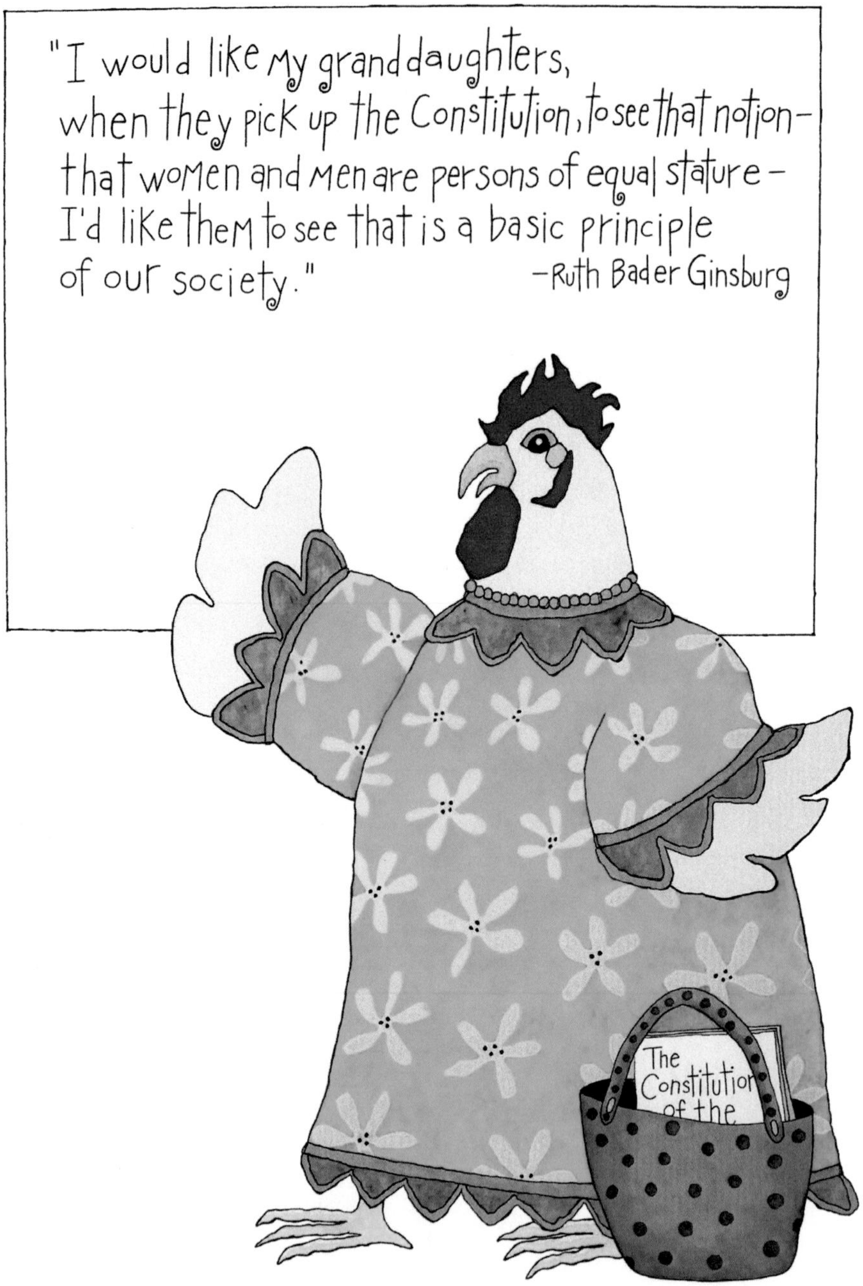
"I would like my granddaughters,
when they pick up the Constitution, to see that notion—
that women and men are persons of equal stature—
I'd like them to see that is a basic principle
of our society."
—Ruth Bader Ginsburg
The
Constitution
of the

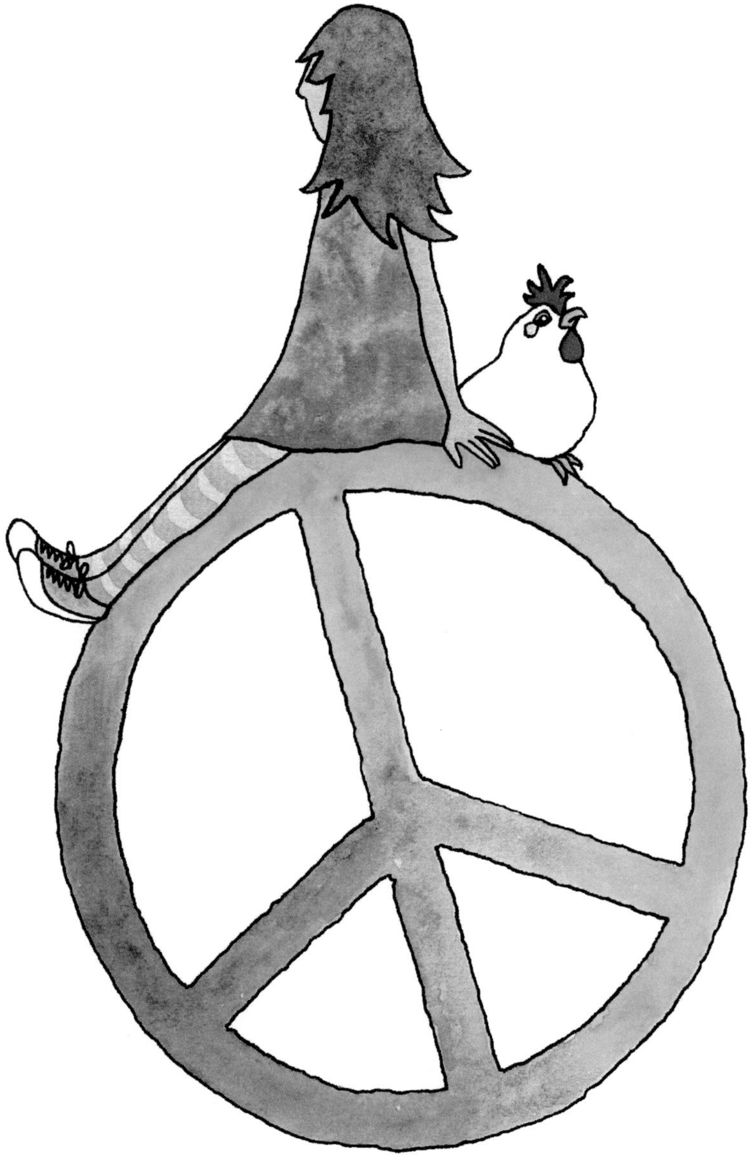

Peace and Hope

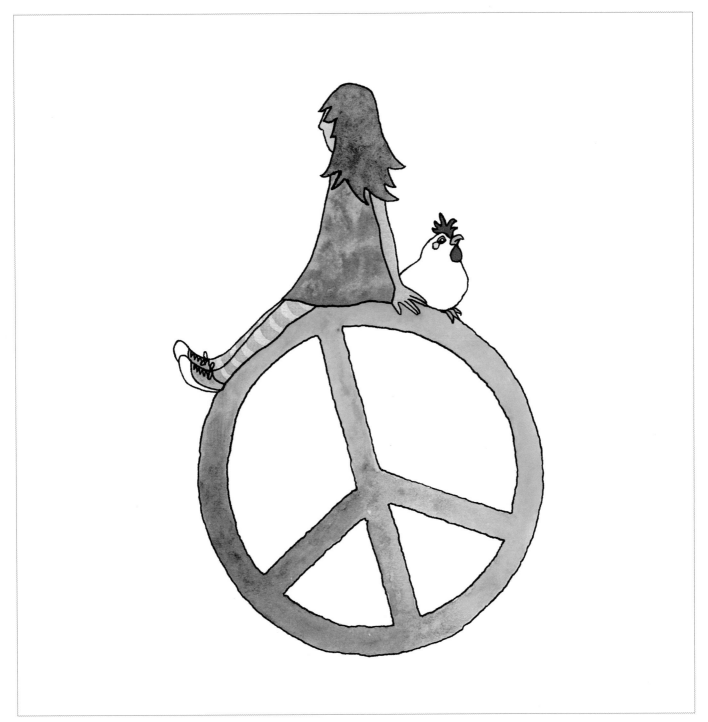

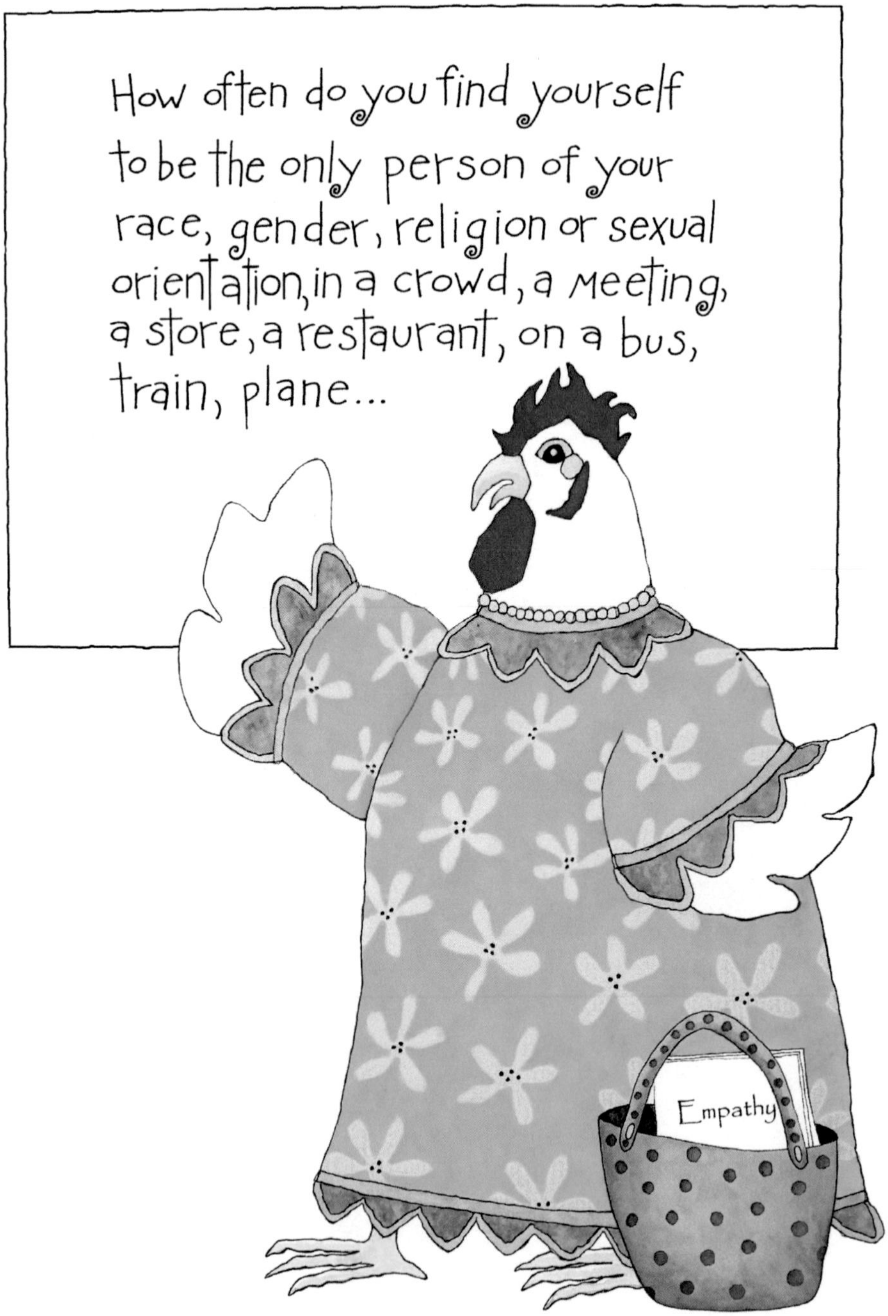
How often do you find yourself to be the only person of your race, gender, religion or sexual orientation, in a crowd, a meeting, a store, a restaurant, on a bus, train, plane...
Empathy

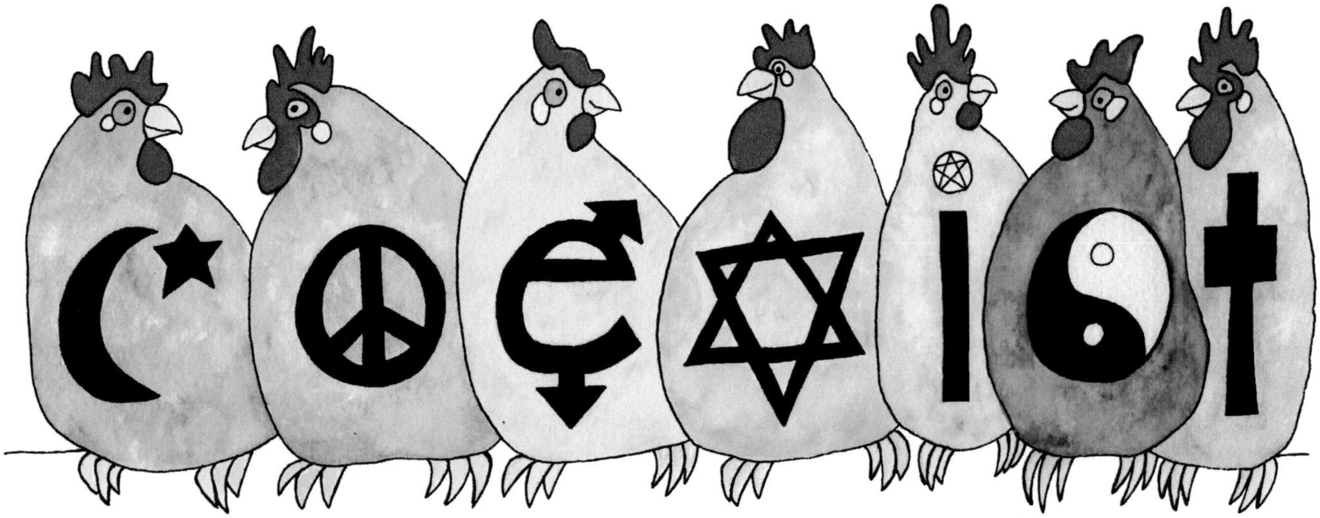

Coexist

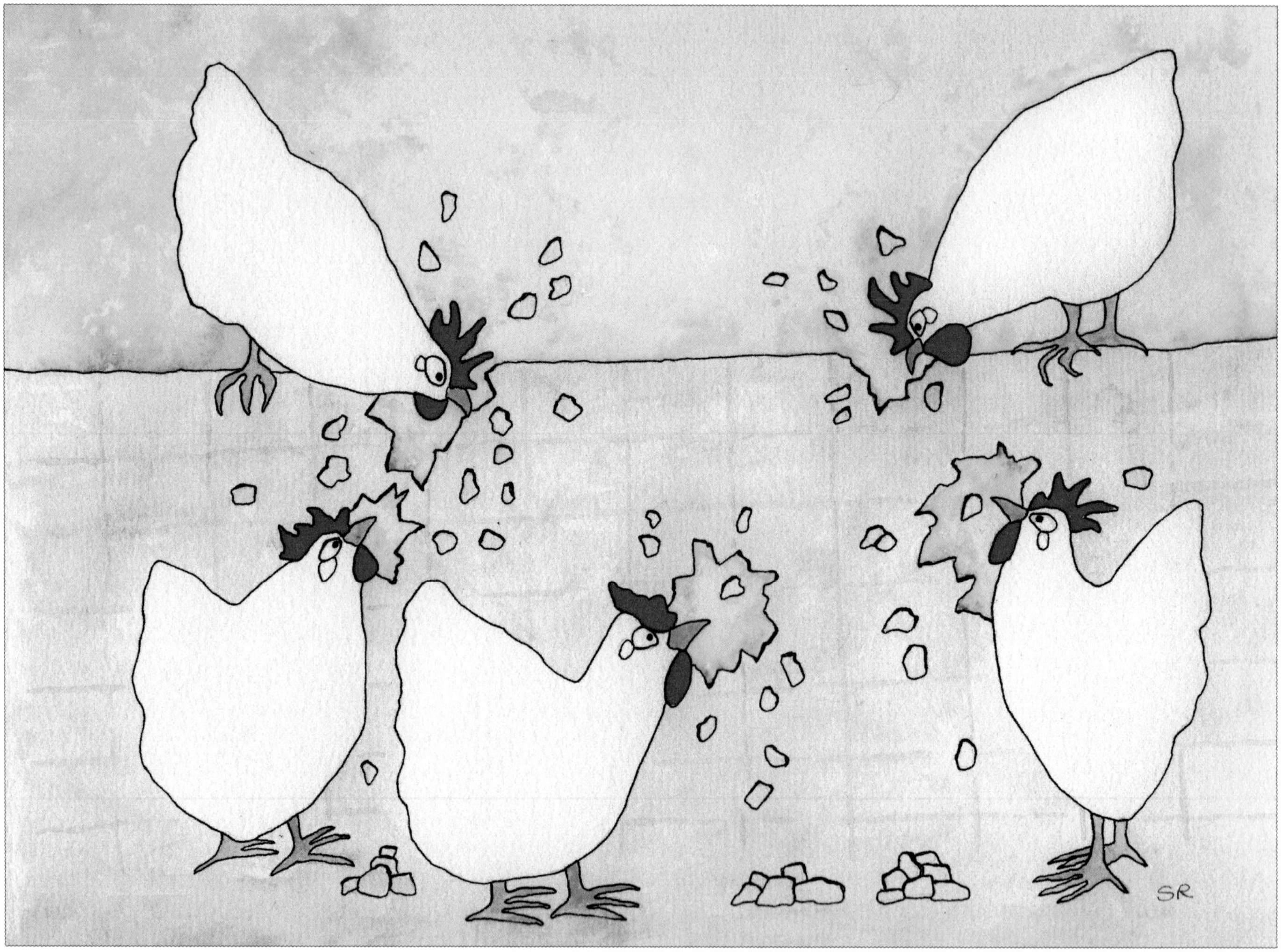
SR

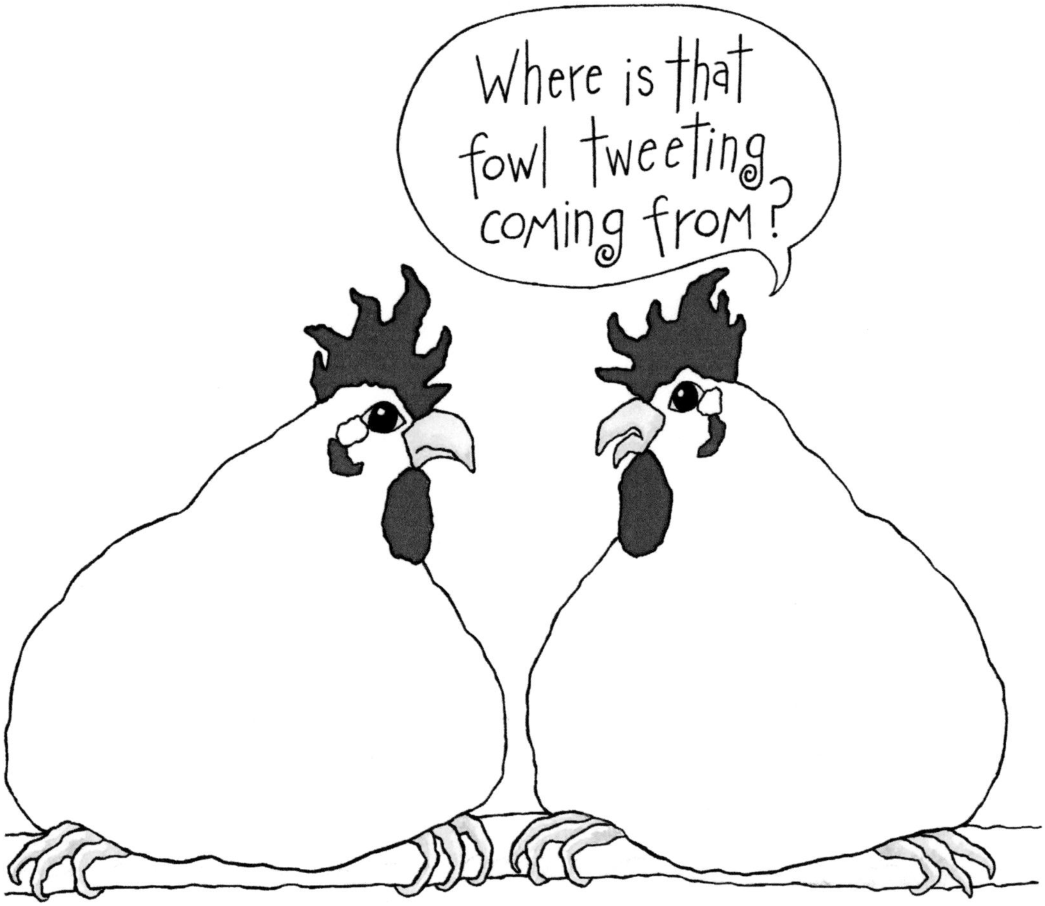
Where is that fowl tweeting coming from?

Tolerance
: sympathy or indulgence for beliefs or practices differing from or conflicting with one's own

All Are Welcome

Power concedes nothing without a demand.
It never did and it never will.

      - Frederick Douglass

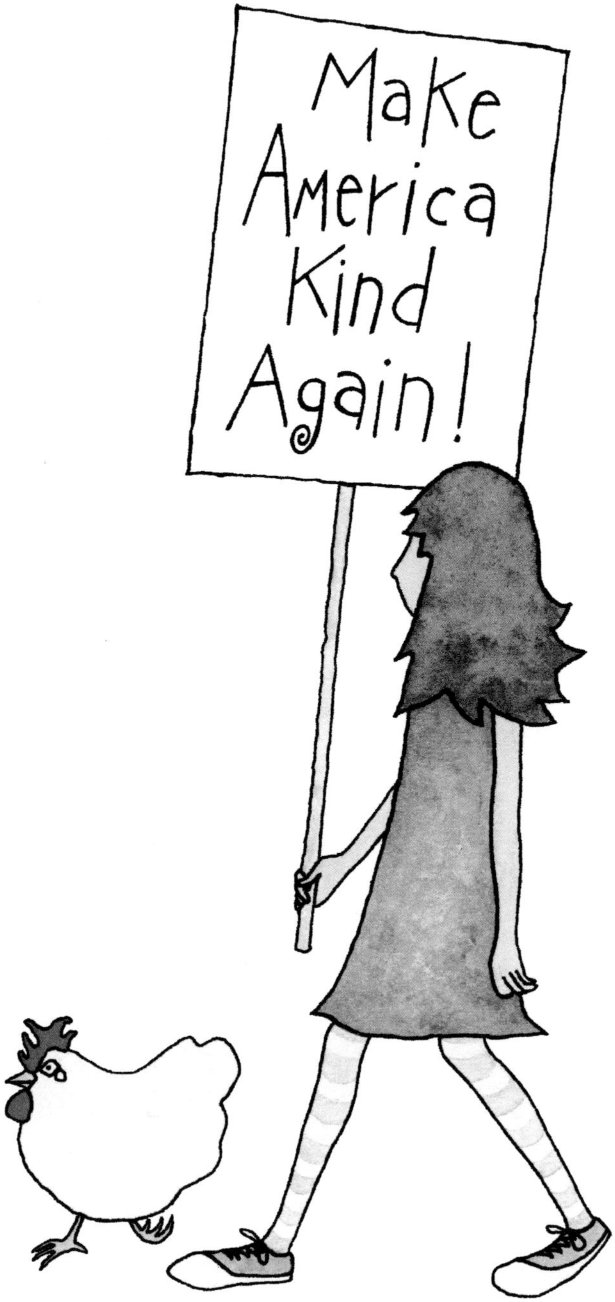
Make
America
Kind
Again!

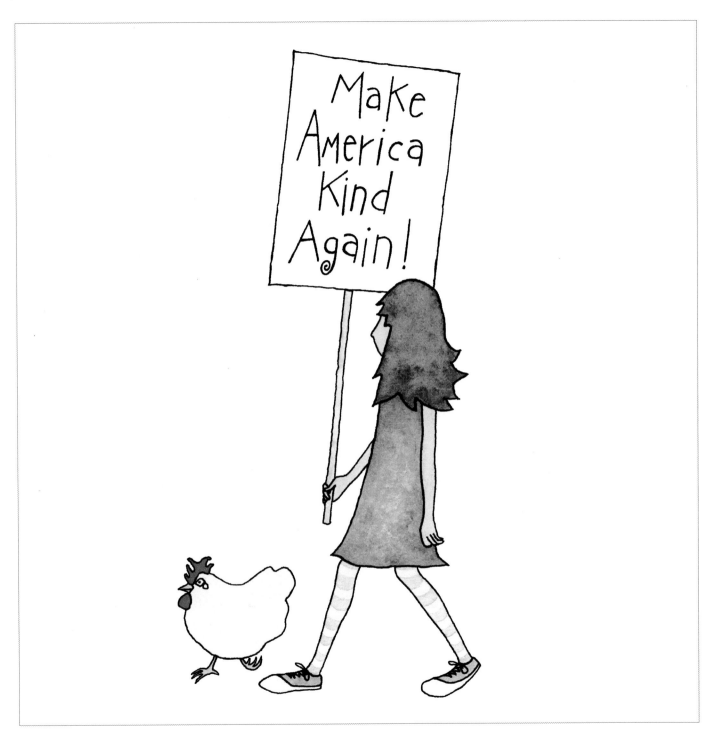

We Can't Hatch a New Earth

EARTH

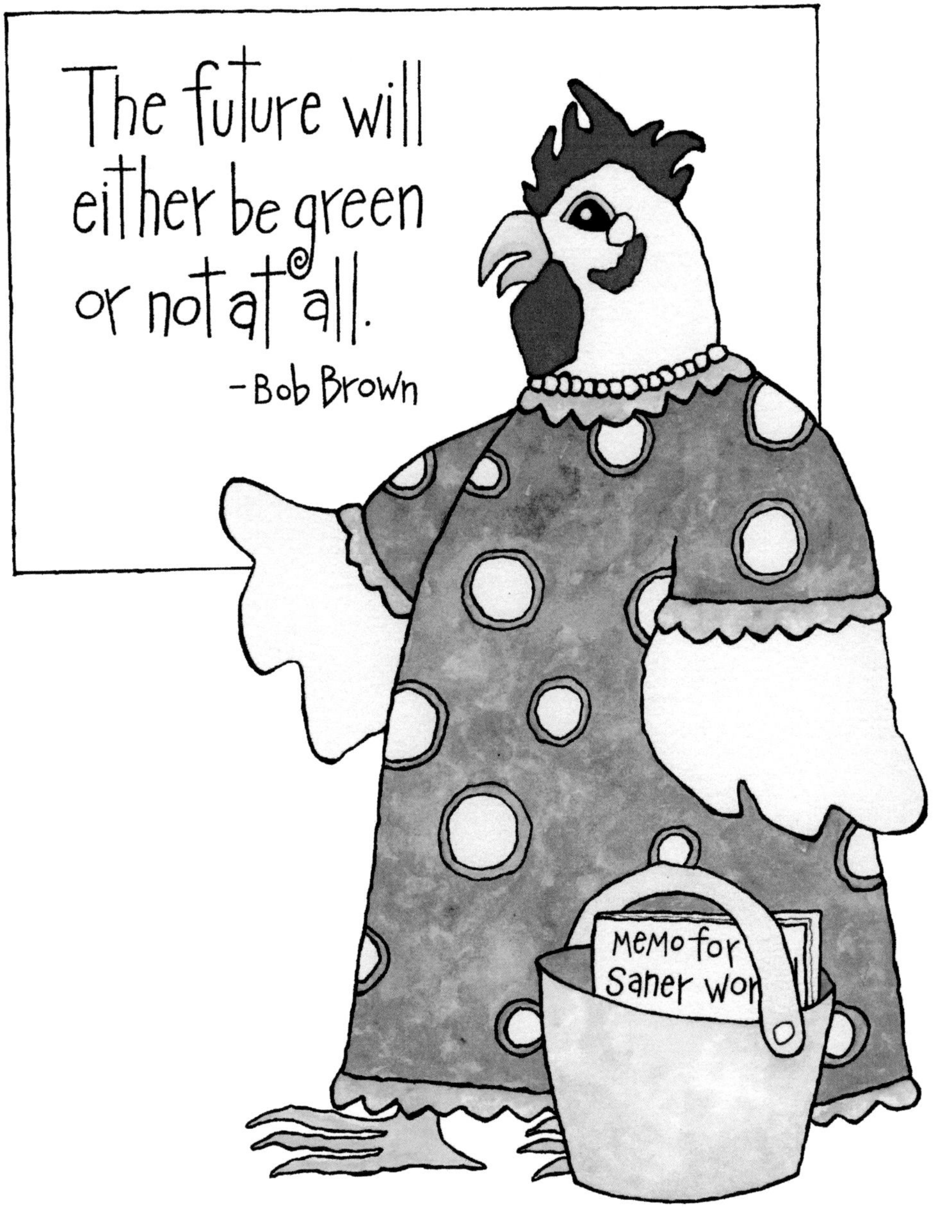
The future will either be green or not at all.
-Bob Brown
MeMo for
Saner wor

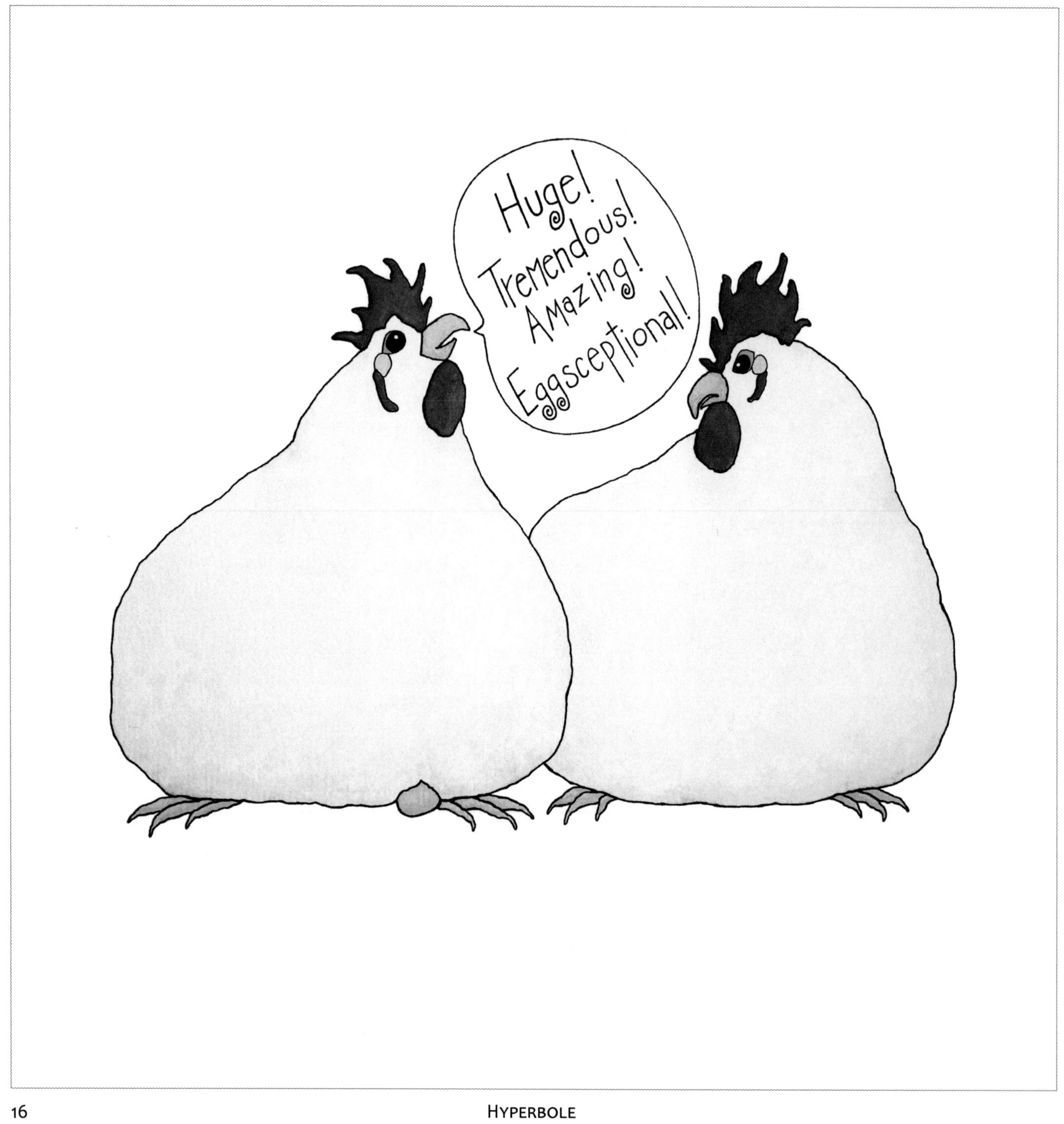
Huge! Tremendous! Amazing! Eggsceptional!

The Surgeon General declares smoking safe, after learning the truth about science.

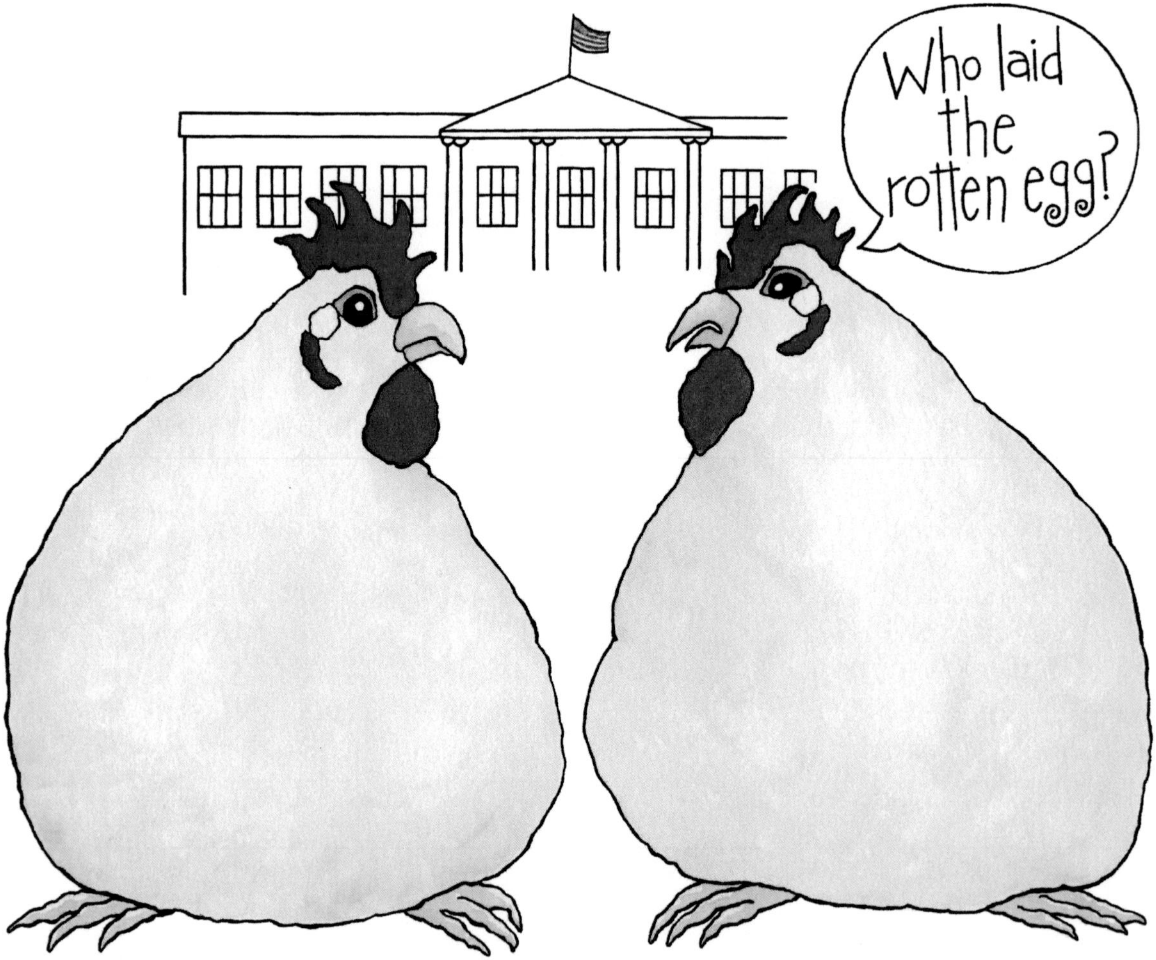
Who laid the rotten egg?

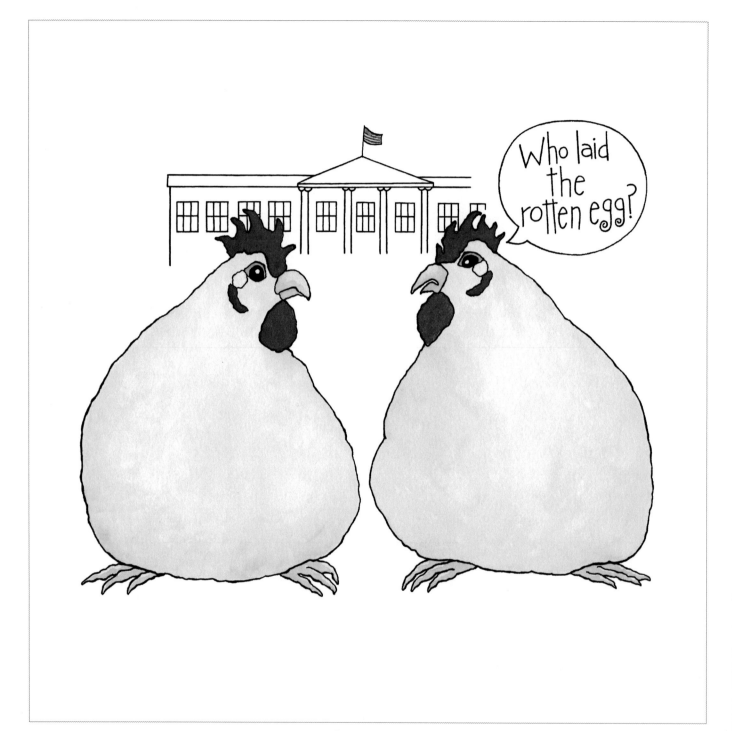

Rotten Egg

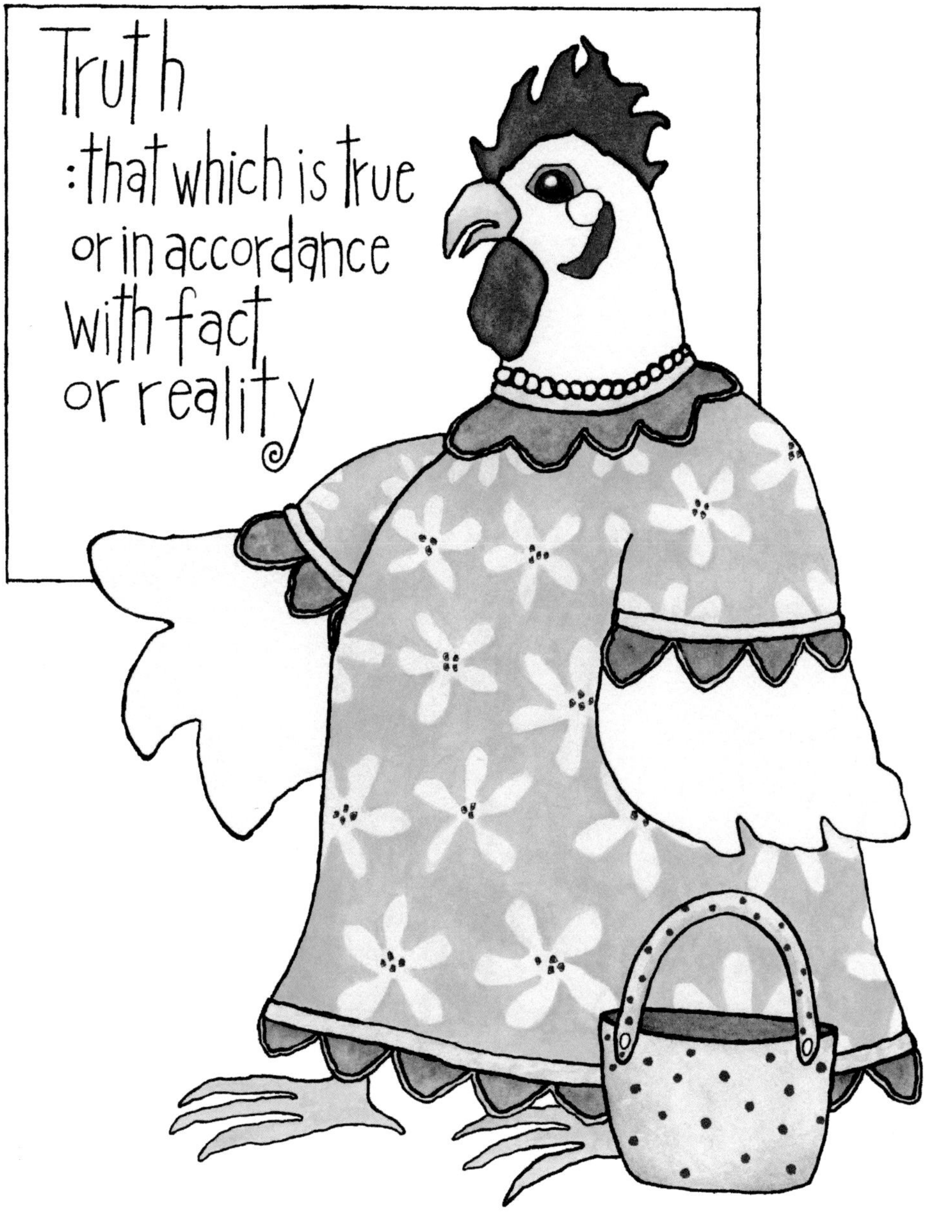
Truth
: that which is true or in accordance with fact or reality

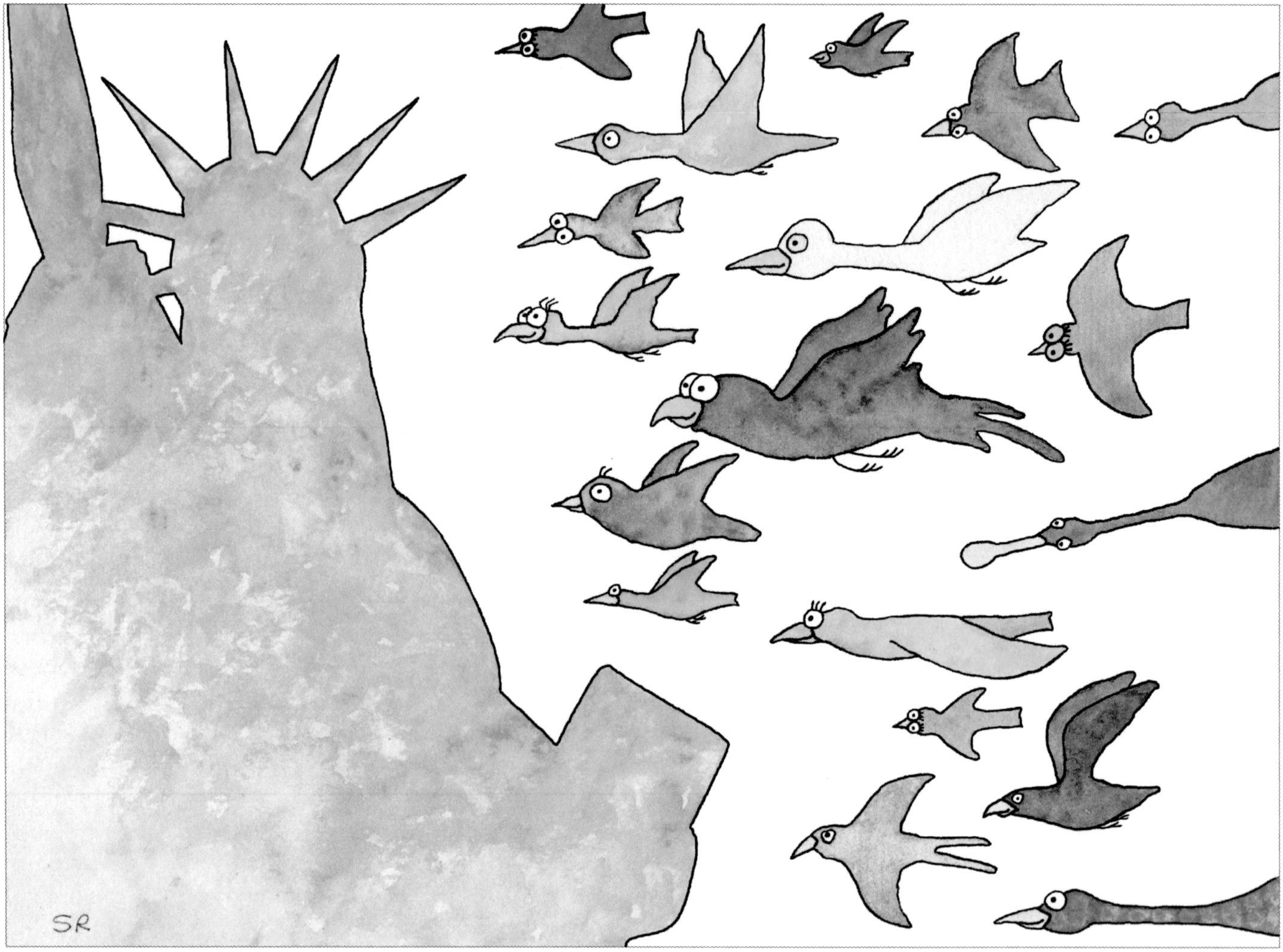
SR

Let's Walk in Someone Else's Shoes

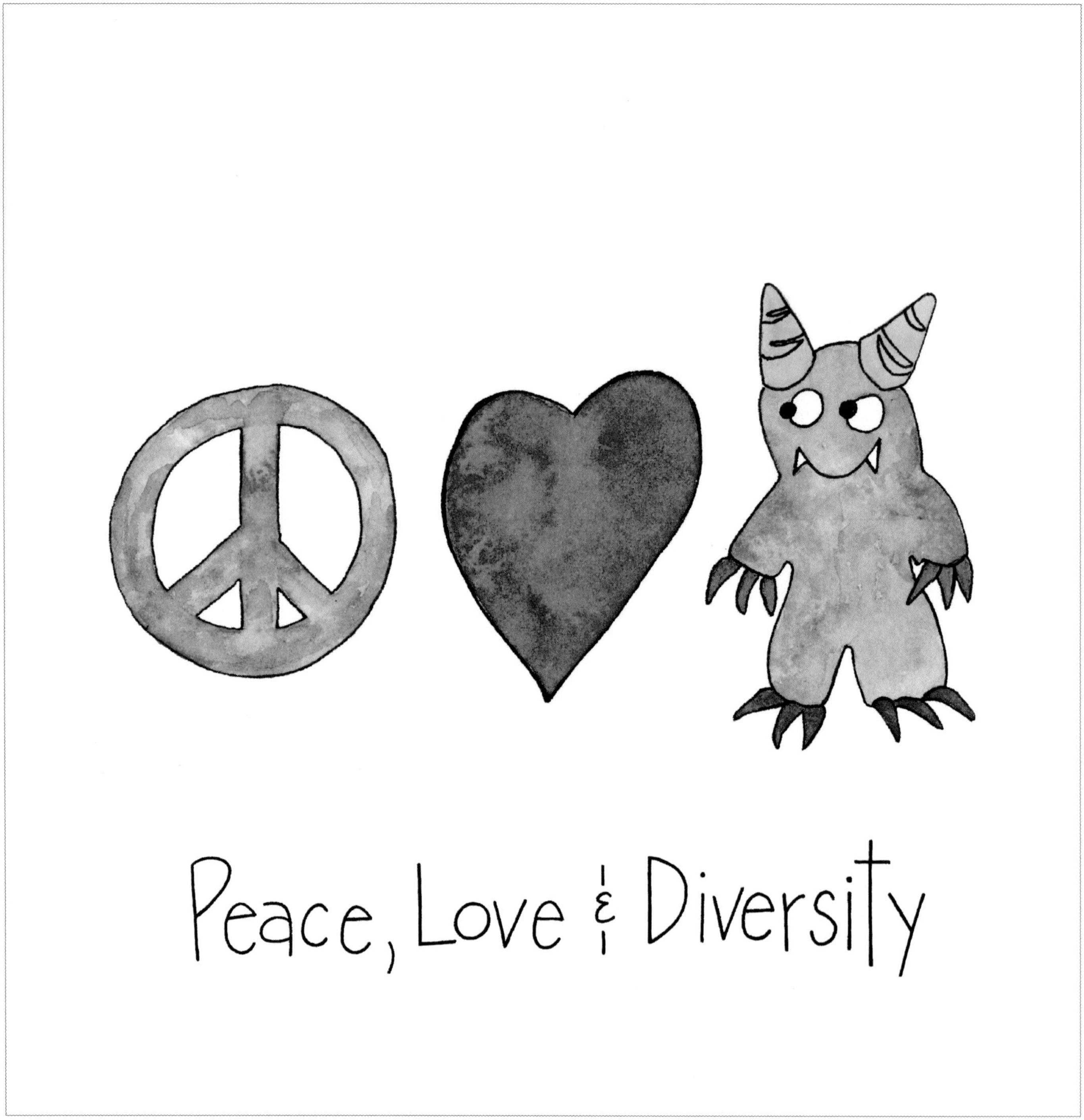
Peace, Love & Diversity

Compassion
  : sympathetic conciousness of others' distress
  together with a desire to alleviate it

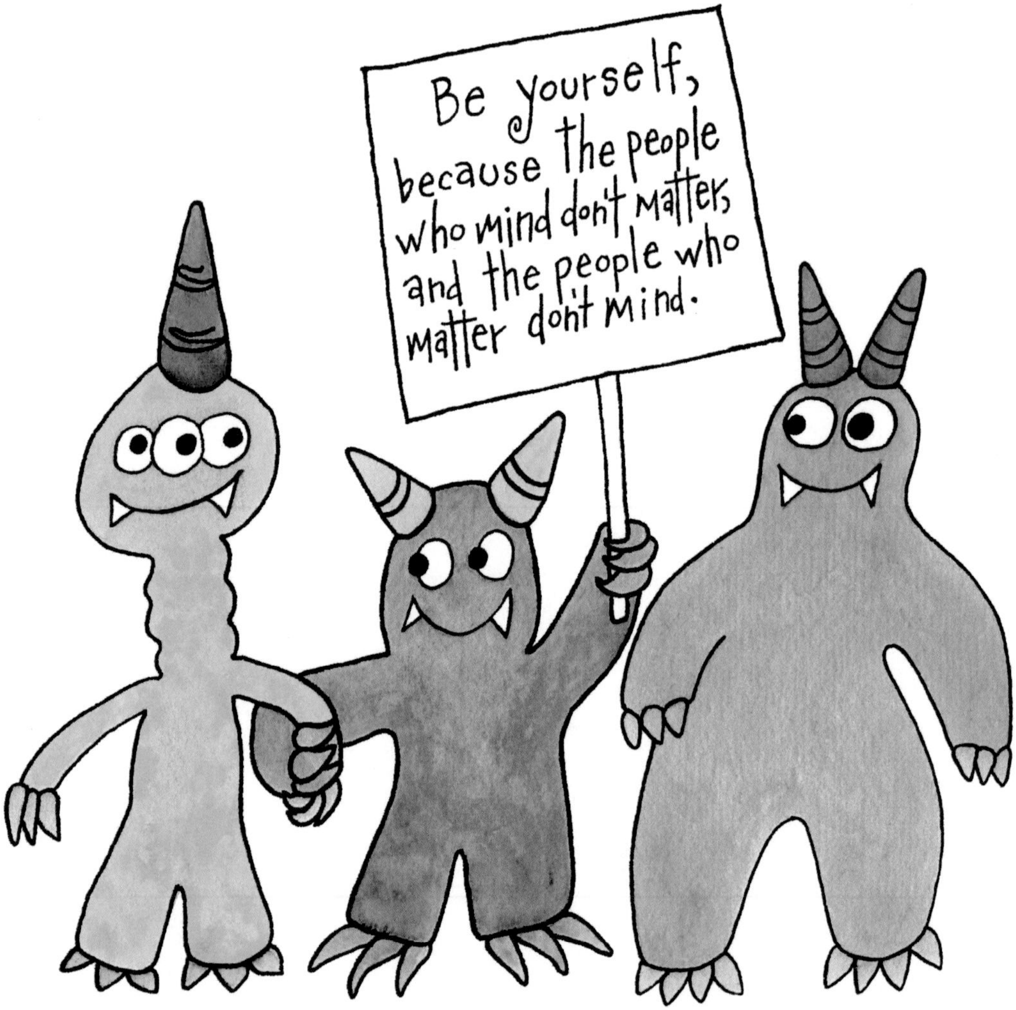
Be yourself,
because the people
who mind don't matter,
and the people who
matter don't mind.

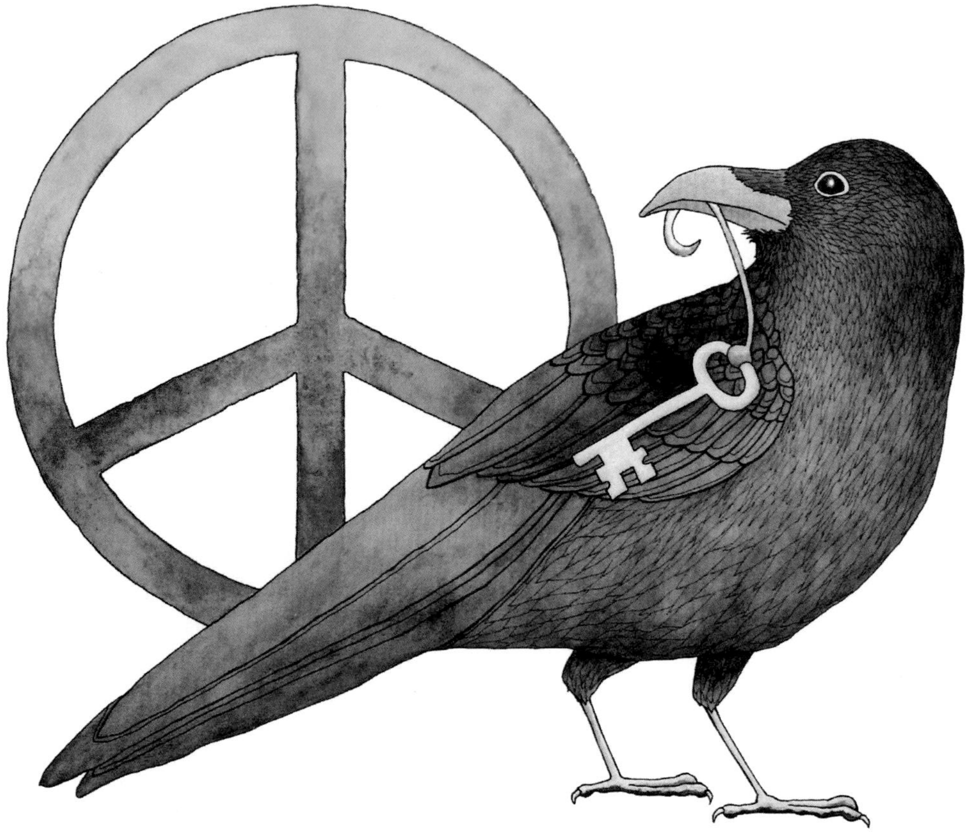

The Messenger

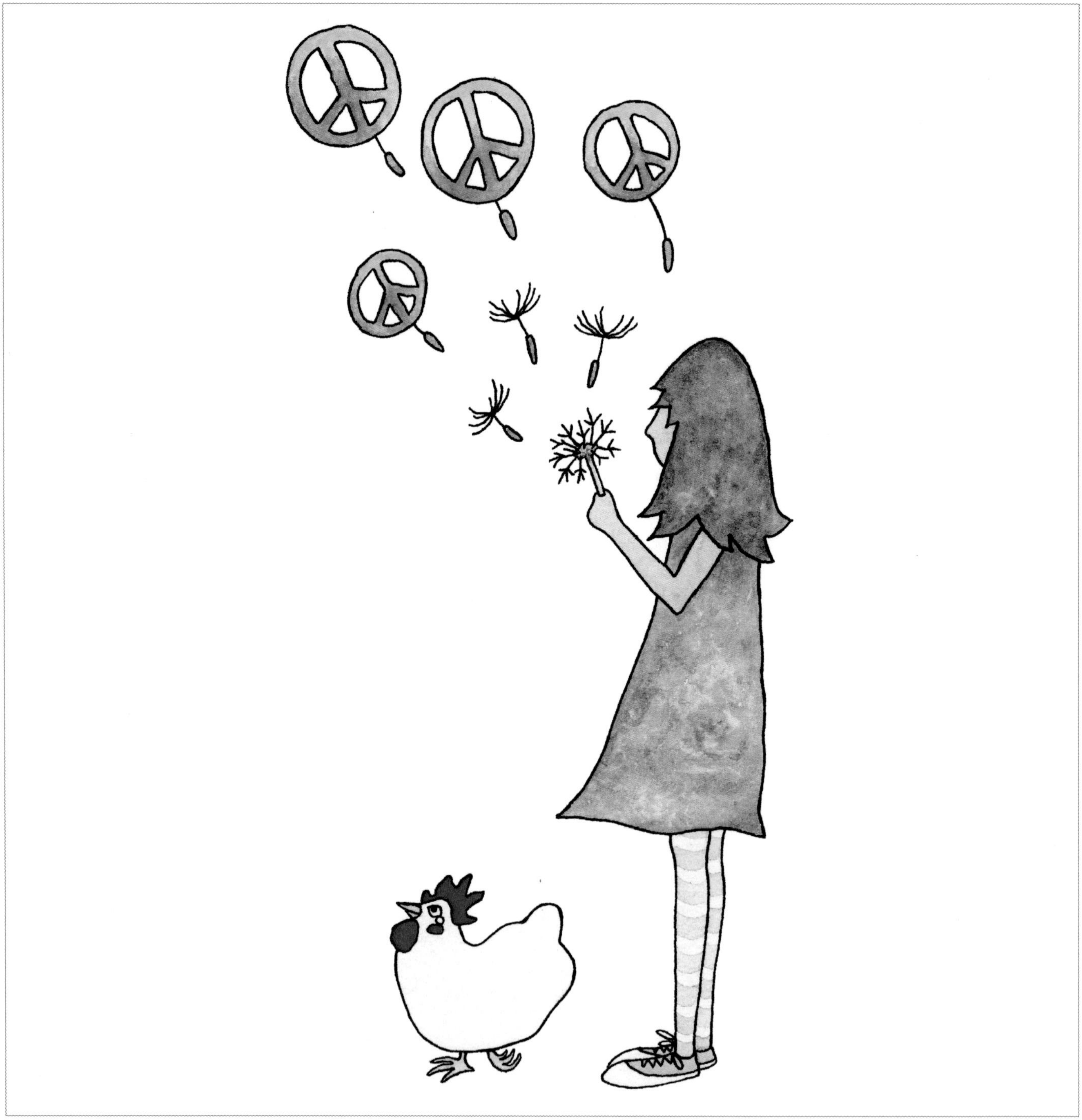

71217983R00018

Made in the USA
Lexington, KY
18 November 2017